十二生肖

Chinese Zodiac

Learn Chinese Calligraphy

Dr. Ping Xu Moroney

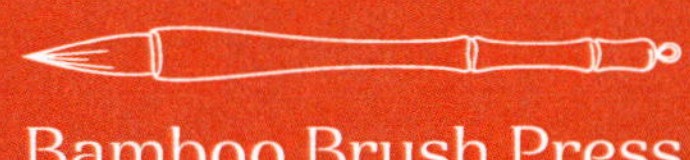

Bamboo Brush Press

Contents

How to Use This Book (The Magic of Tracing)

The process is intuitive and meditative:

1. Place a Sheet: Simply place a thin piece of white practice paper (like tracing paper or calligraphy paper) over the page in the book.

2. Trace the Master: Clearly visible through the paper, you will see the faint, guide-like image of a zodiac character (e.g., 牛 for Ox, 虎 for Tiger).

3. Follow the Flow: Using a brush pen, fountain pen, or even a marker, trace over the guide. Focus on replicating the pressure (thick and thin parts) of each stroke.

4. Learn and Repeat: Practice each character multiple times to build muscle memory and confidence. Before you know it, you'll be drawing the characters for all 12 zodiac animals-鼠, 虎, 兔, 龙, 蛇, 马, 羊, 猴, 鸡, 狗, 猪-with grace and skill.

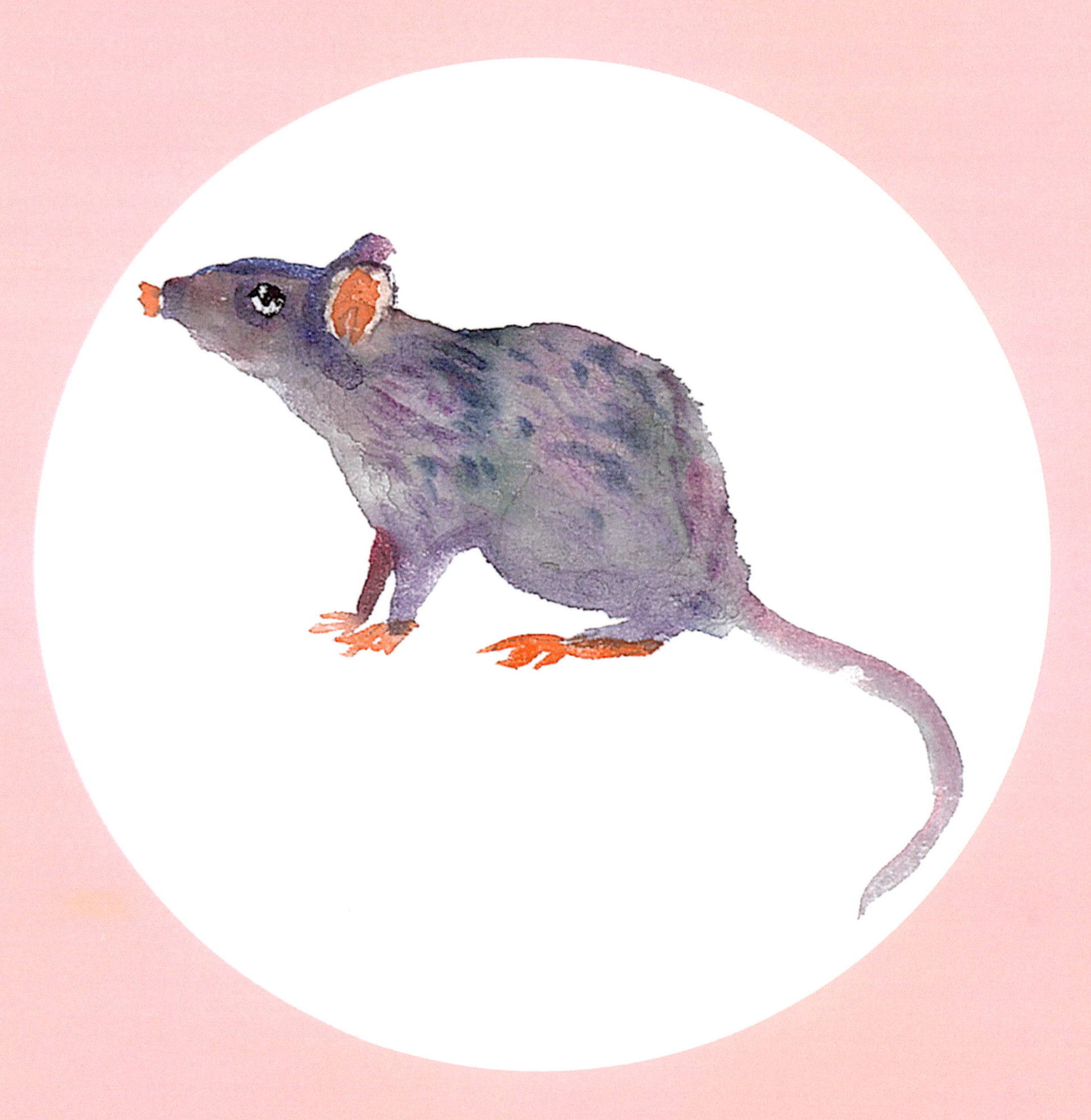

Shǔ Rat

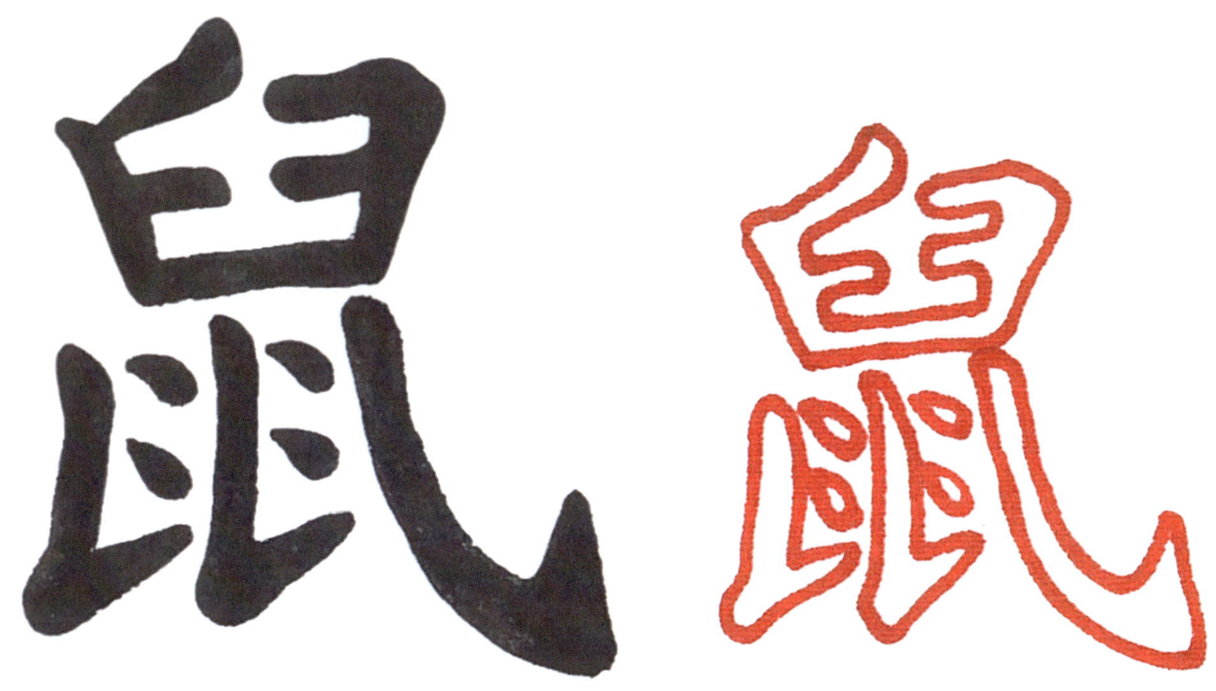

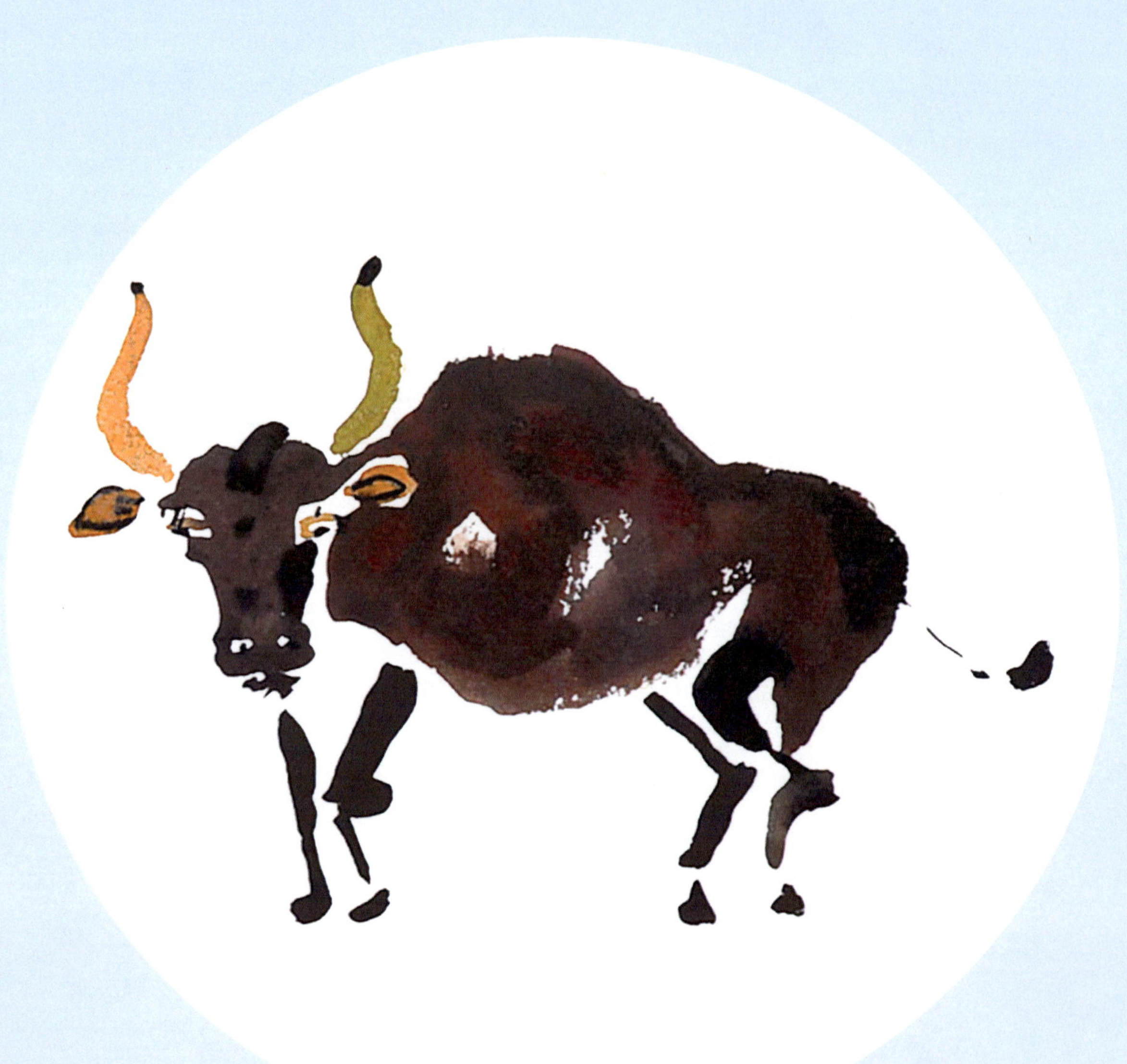

Niú Ox

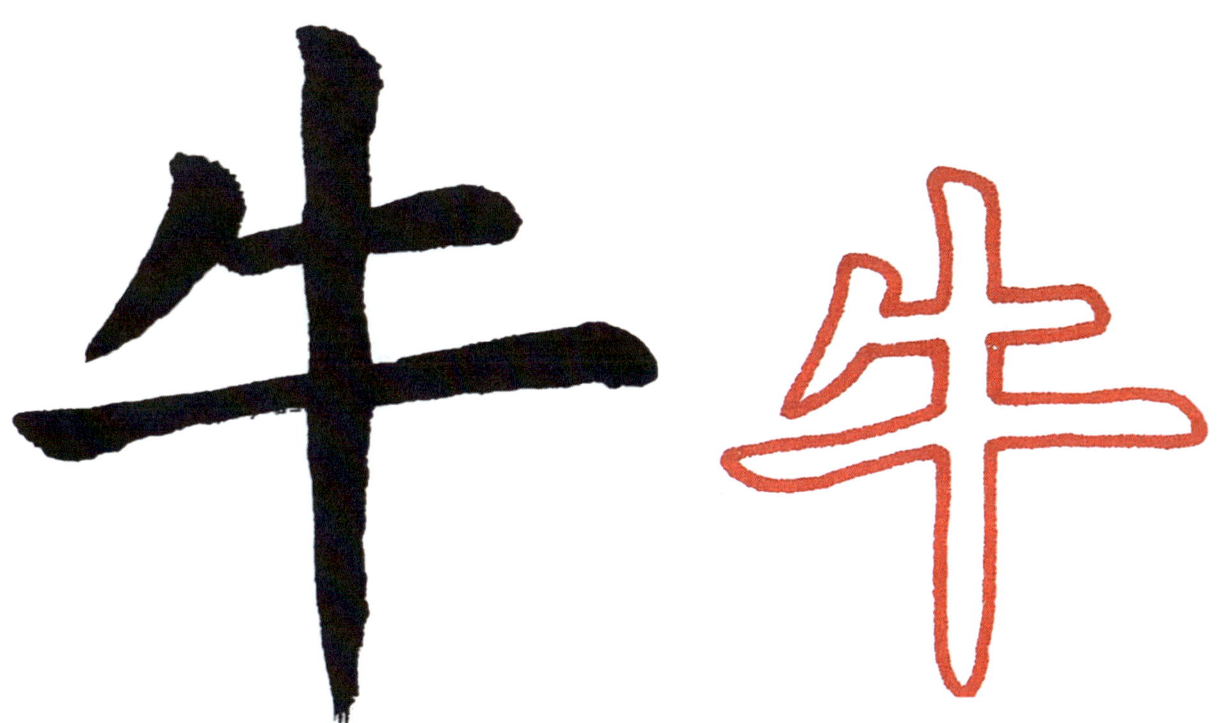

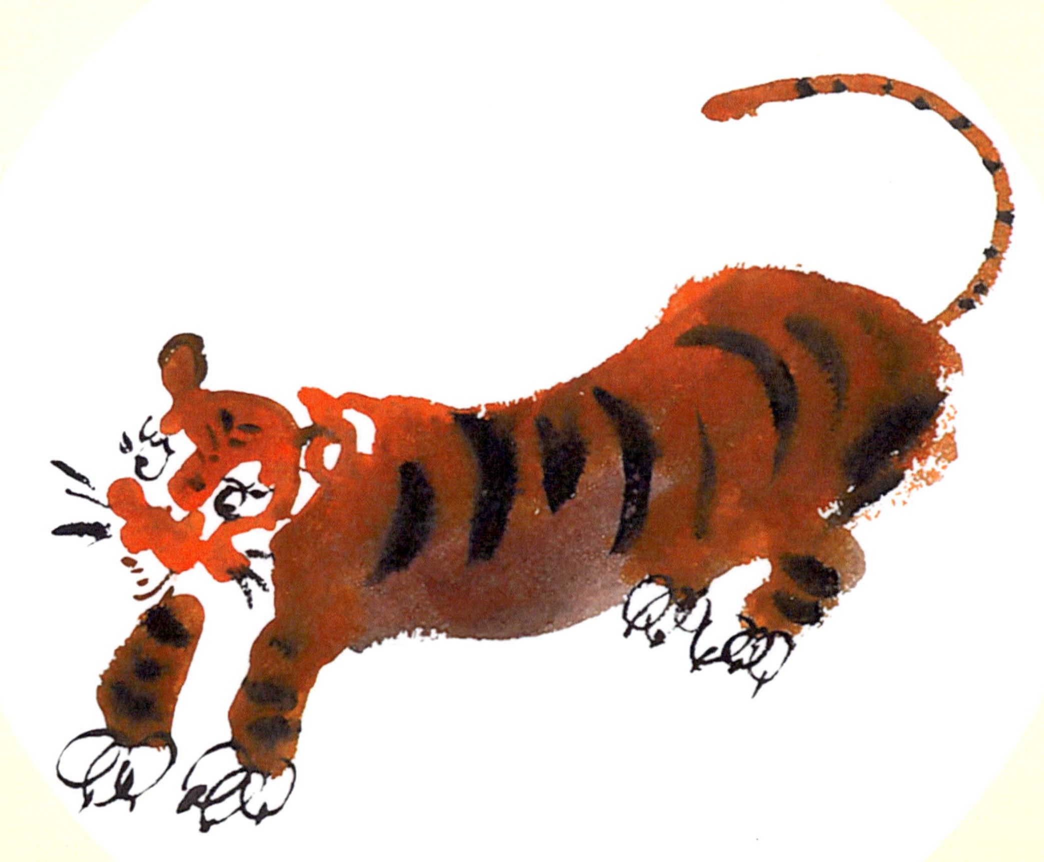

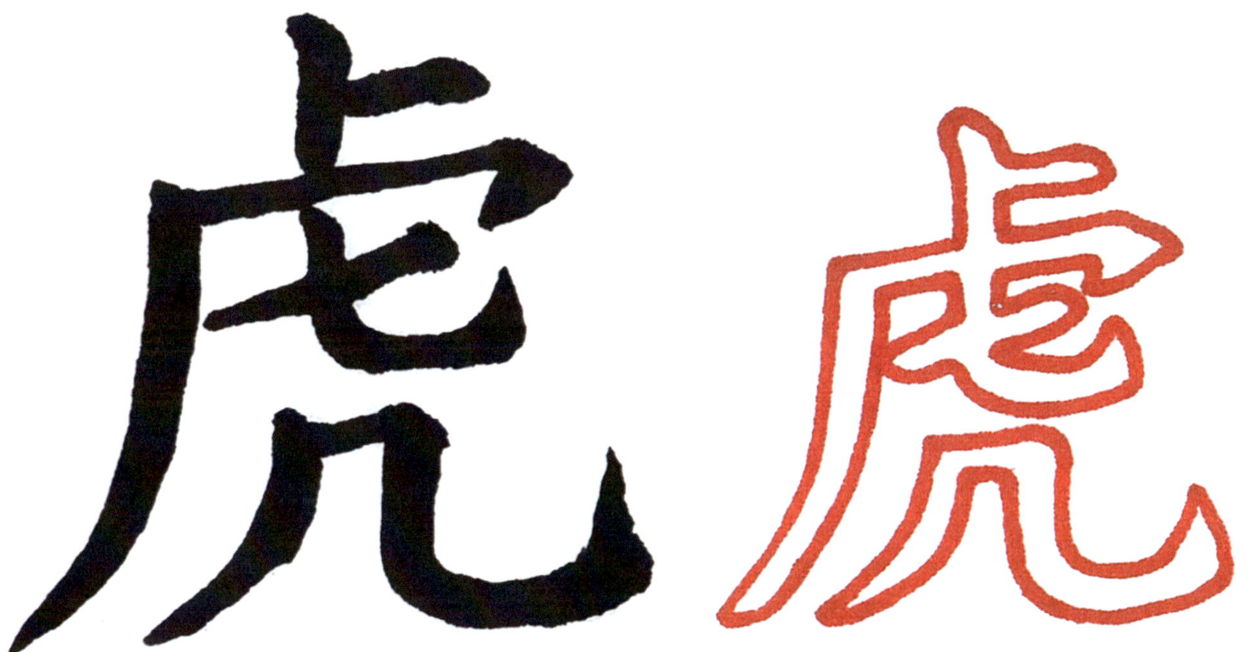

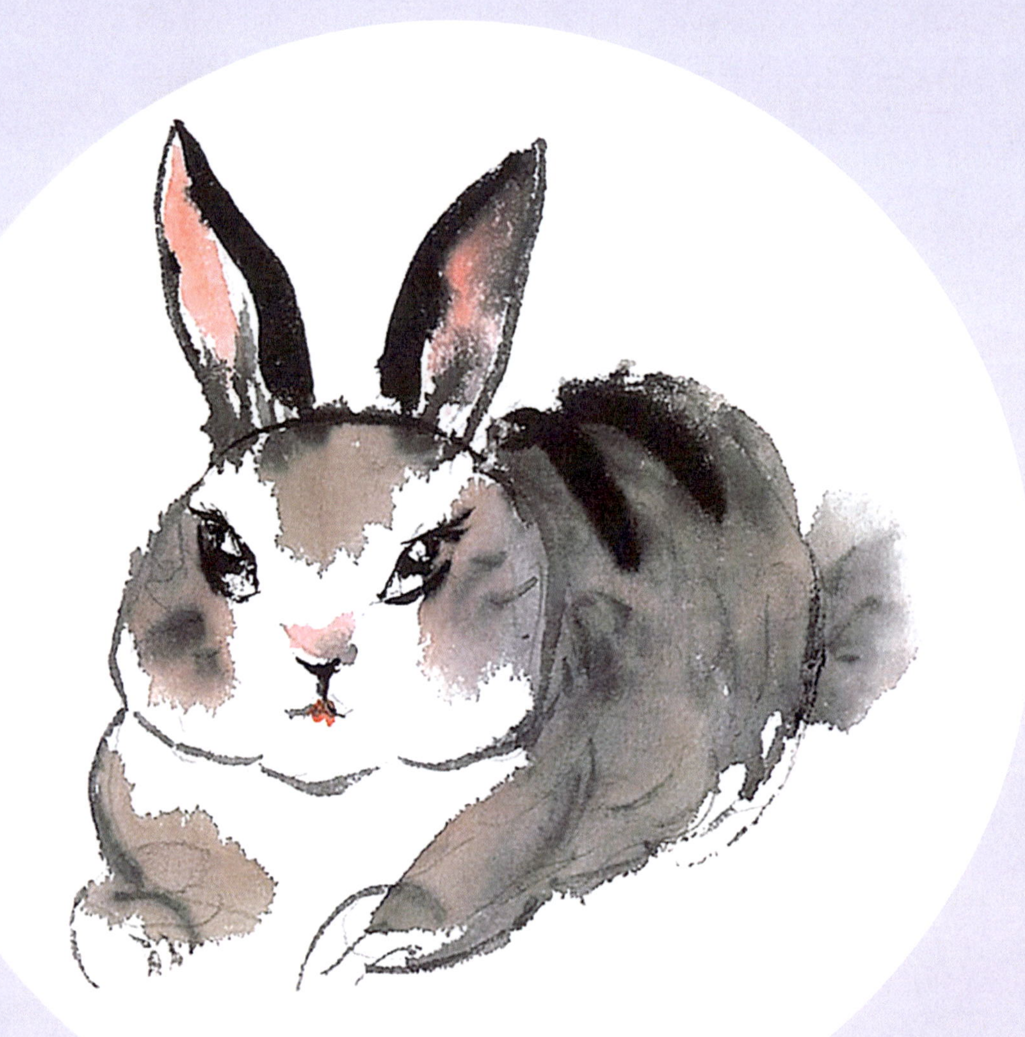

Tù Rabbit

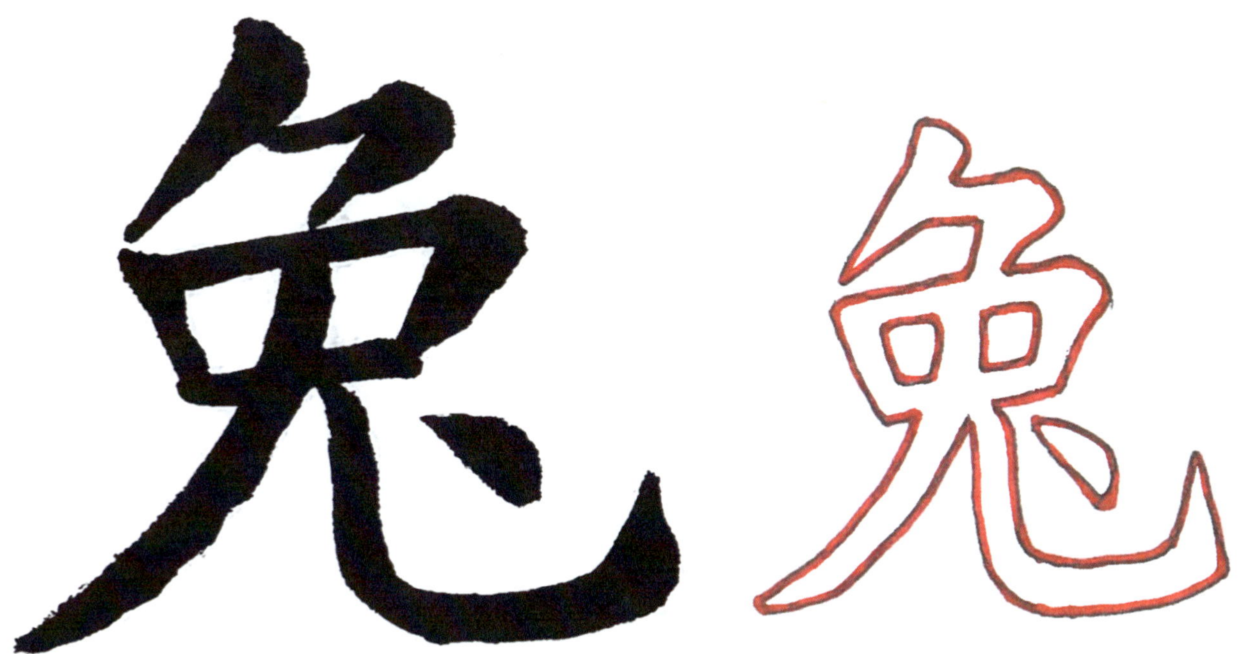

11

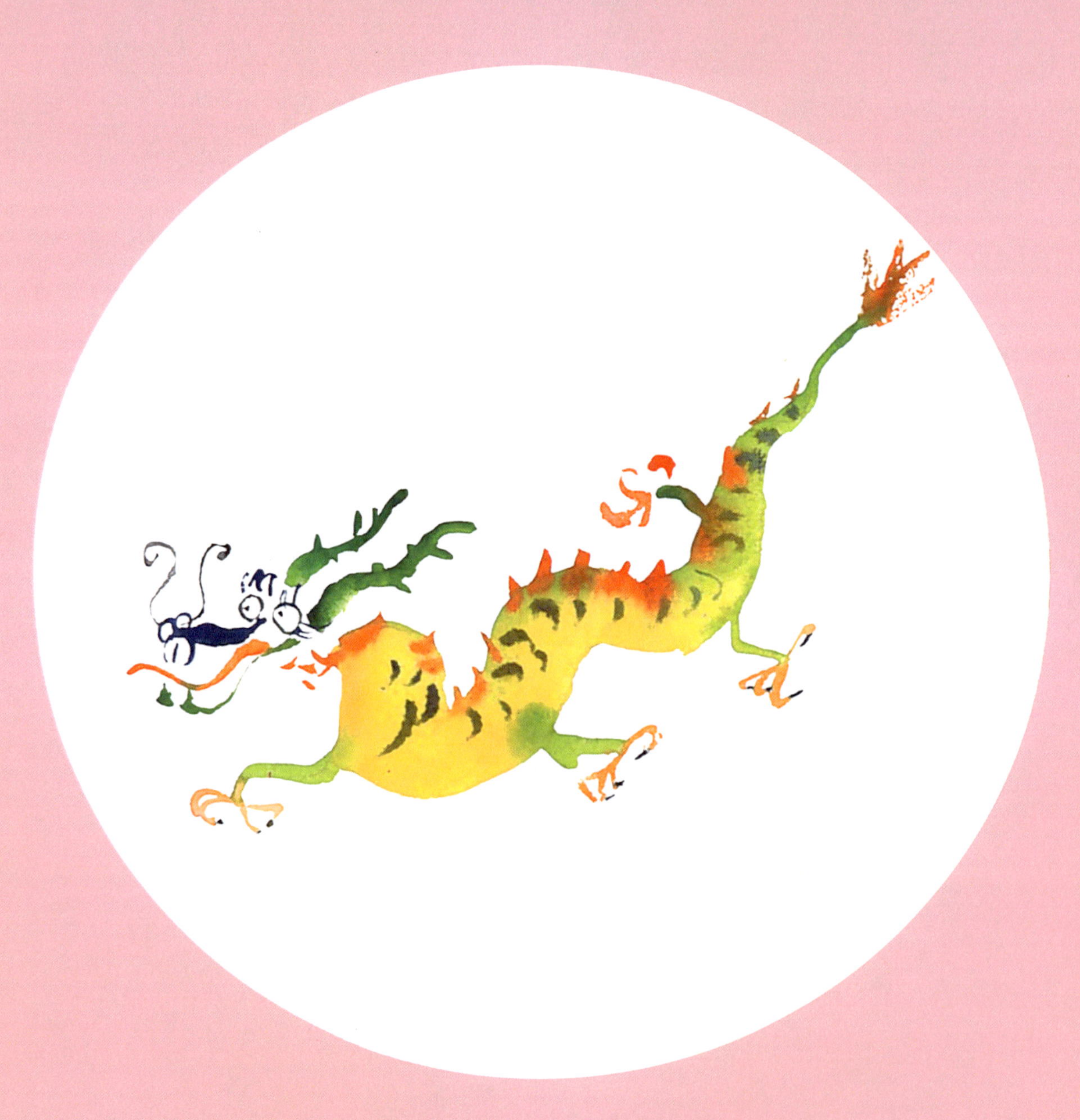

Lóng Dragon

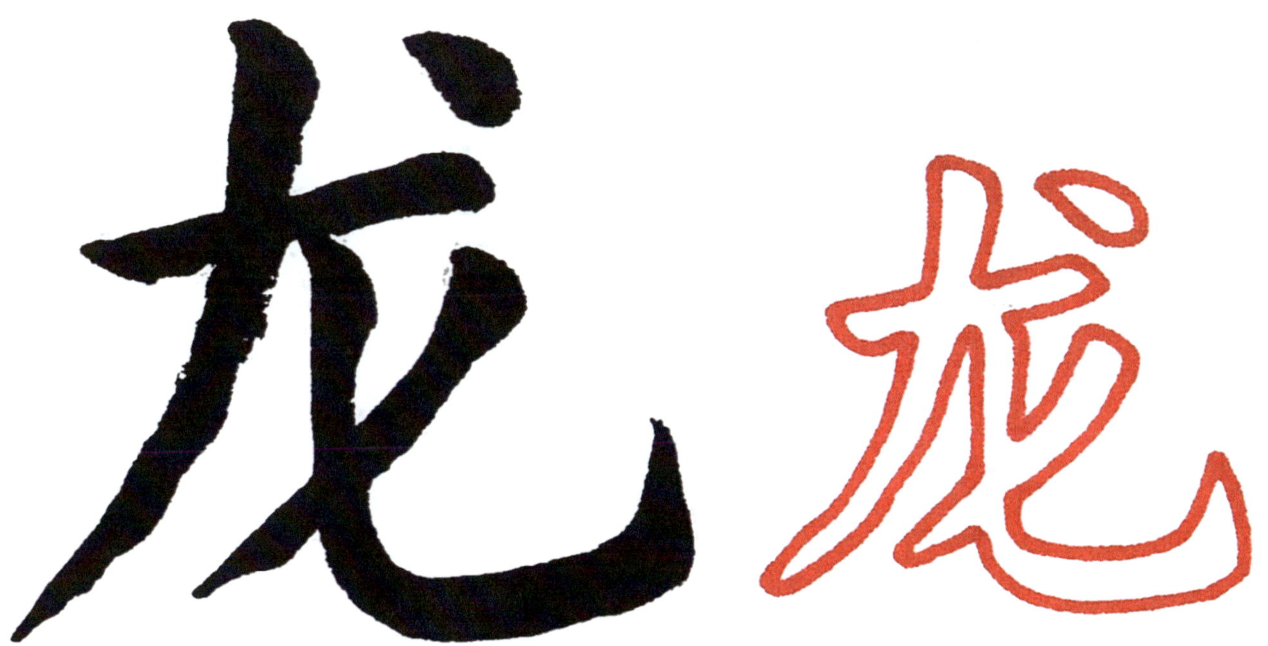

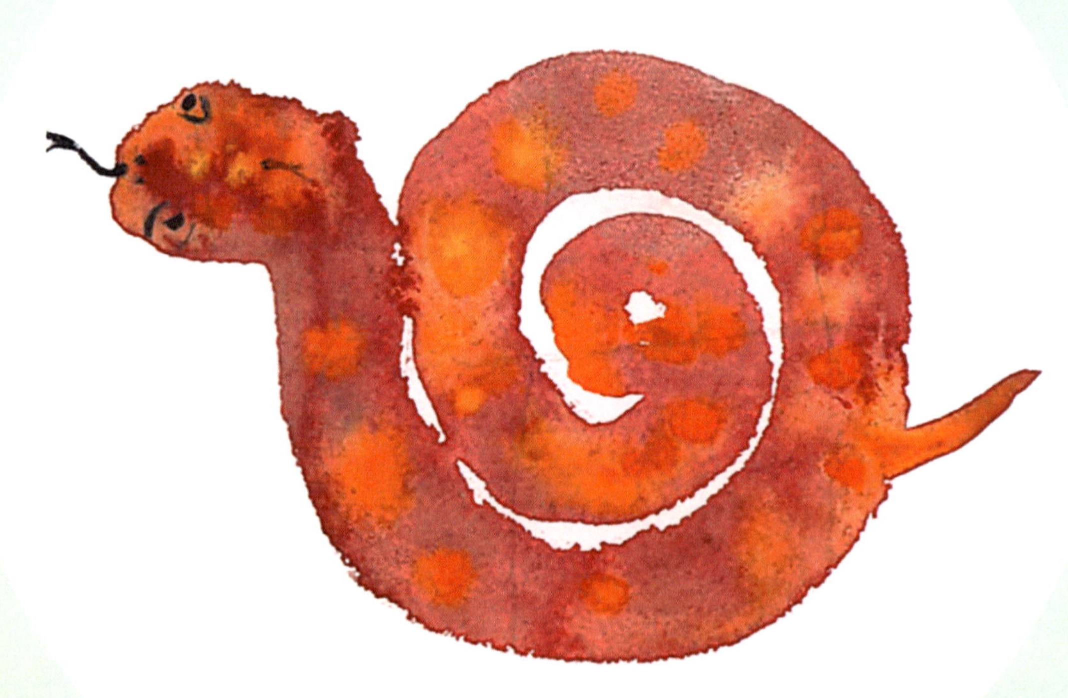

Shé Snake

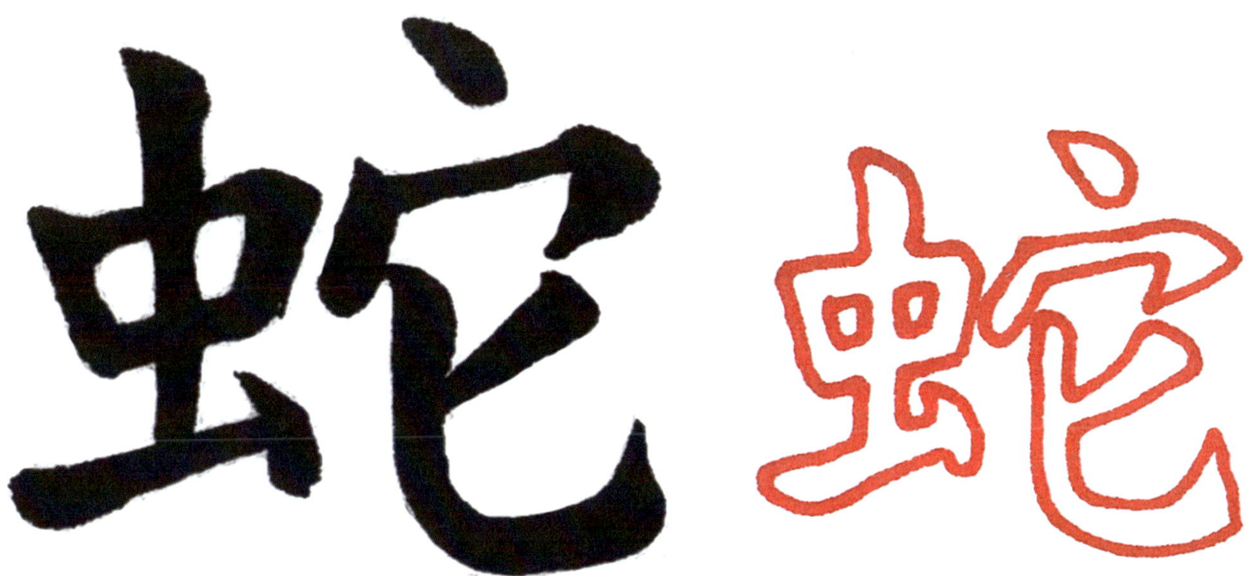

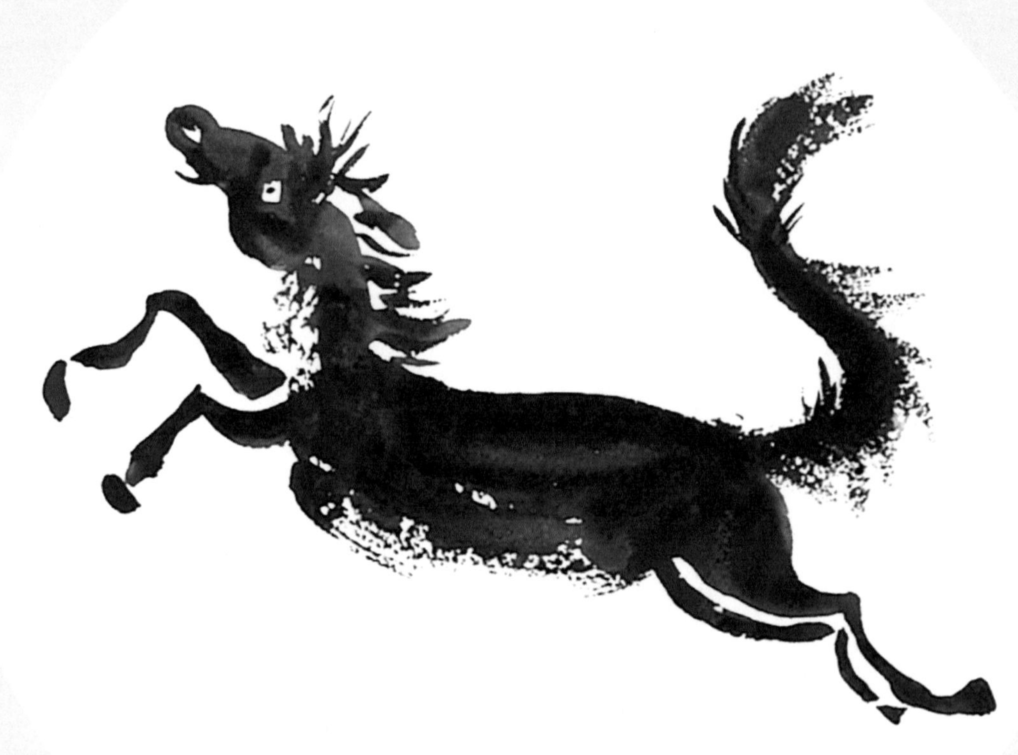

Mǎ Horse

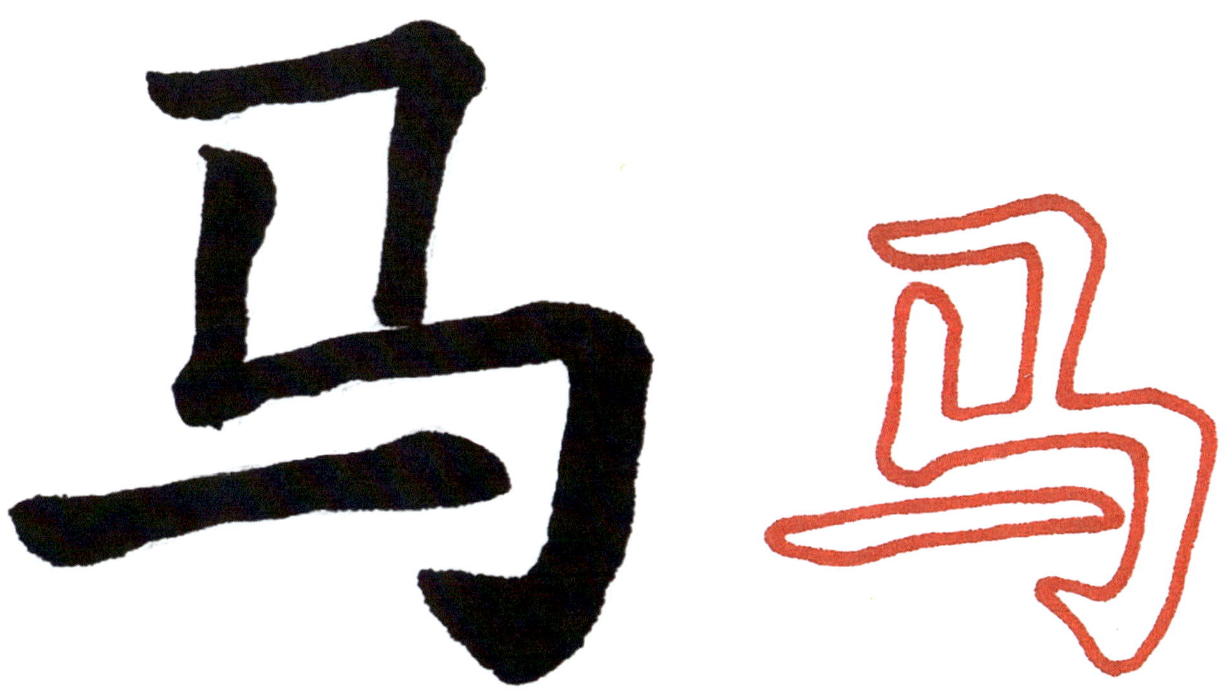

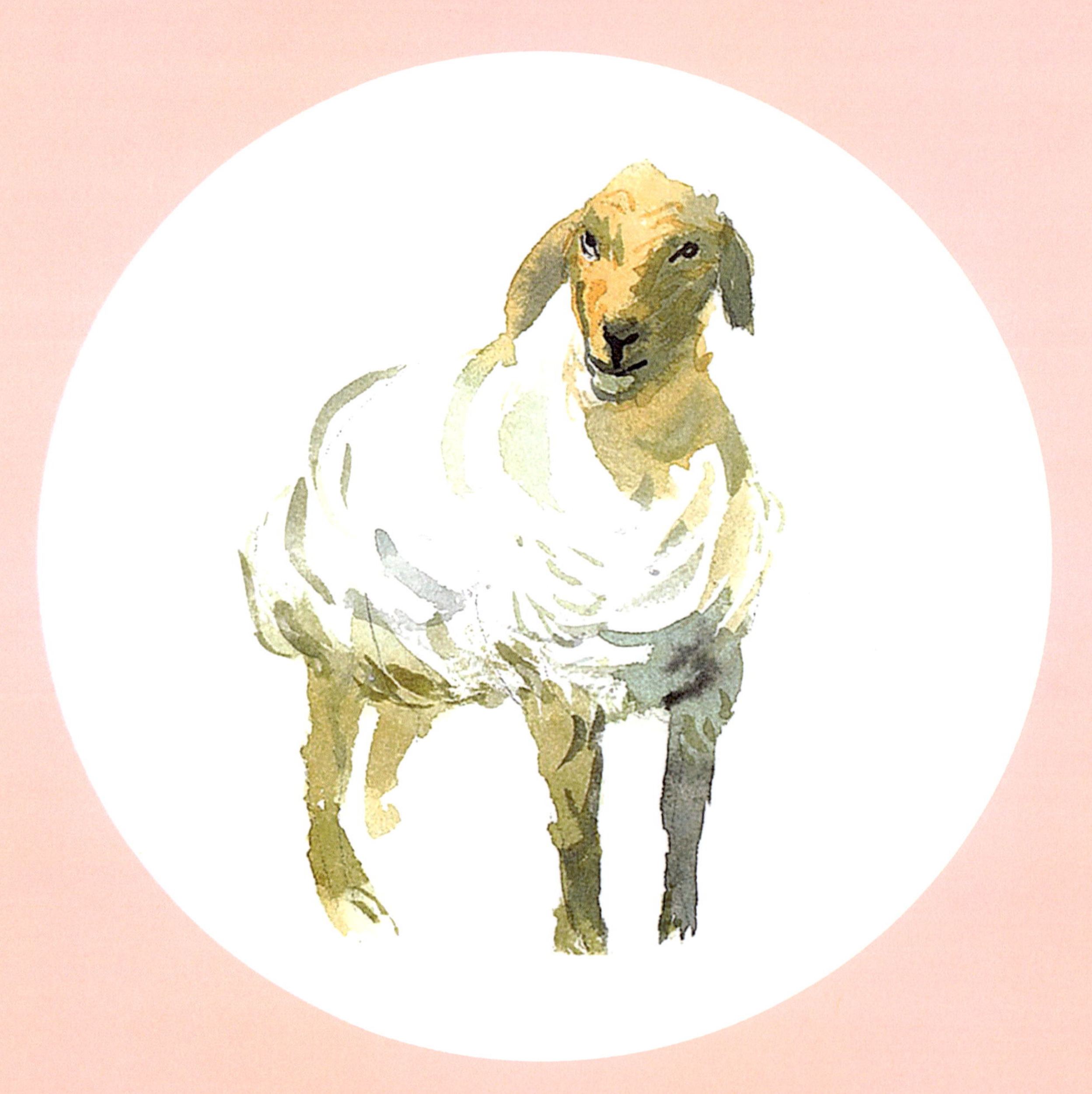

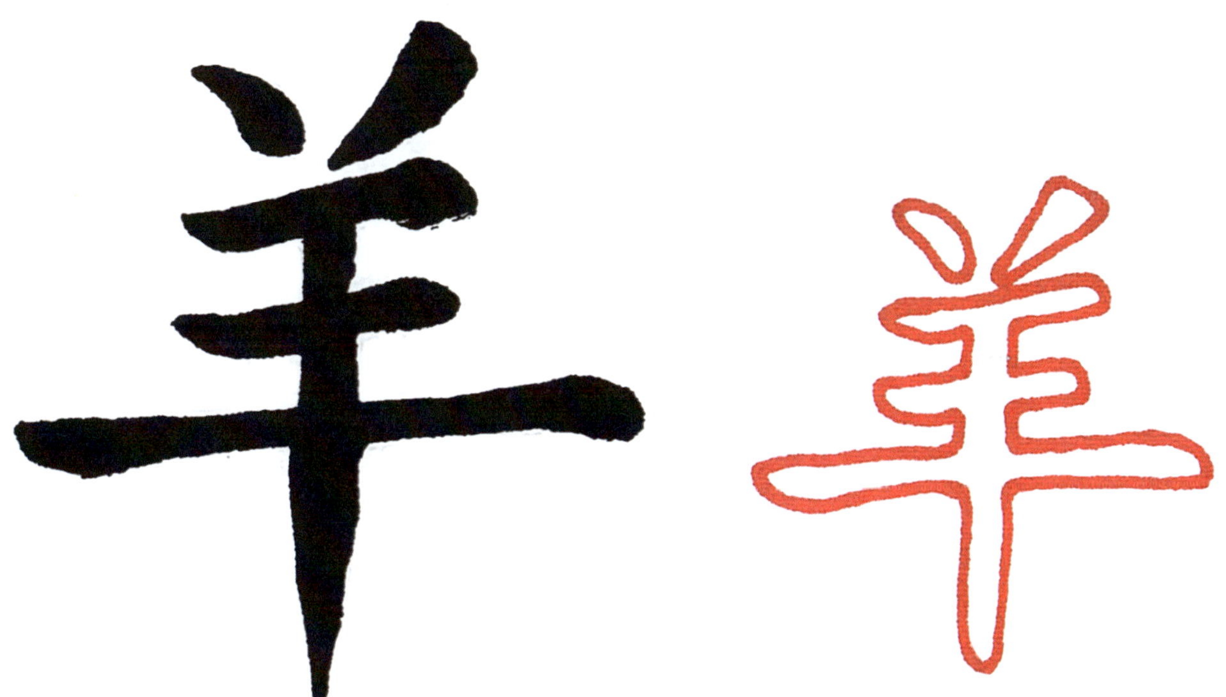

19

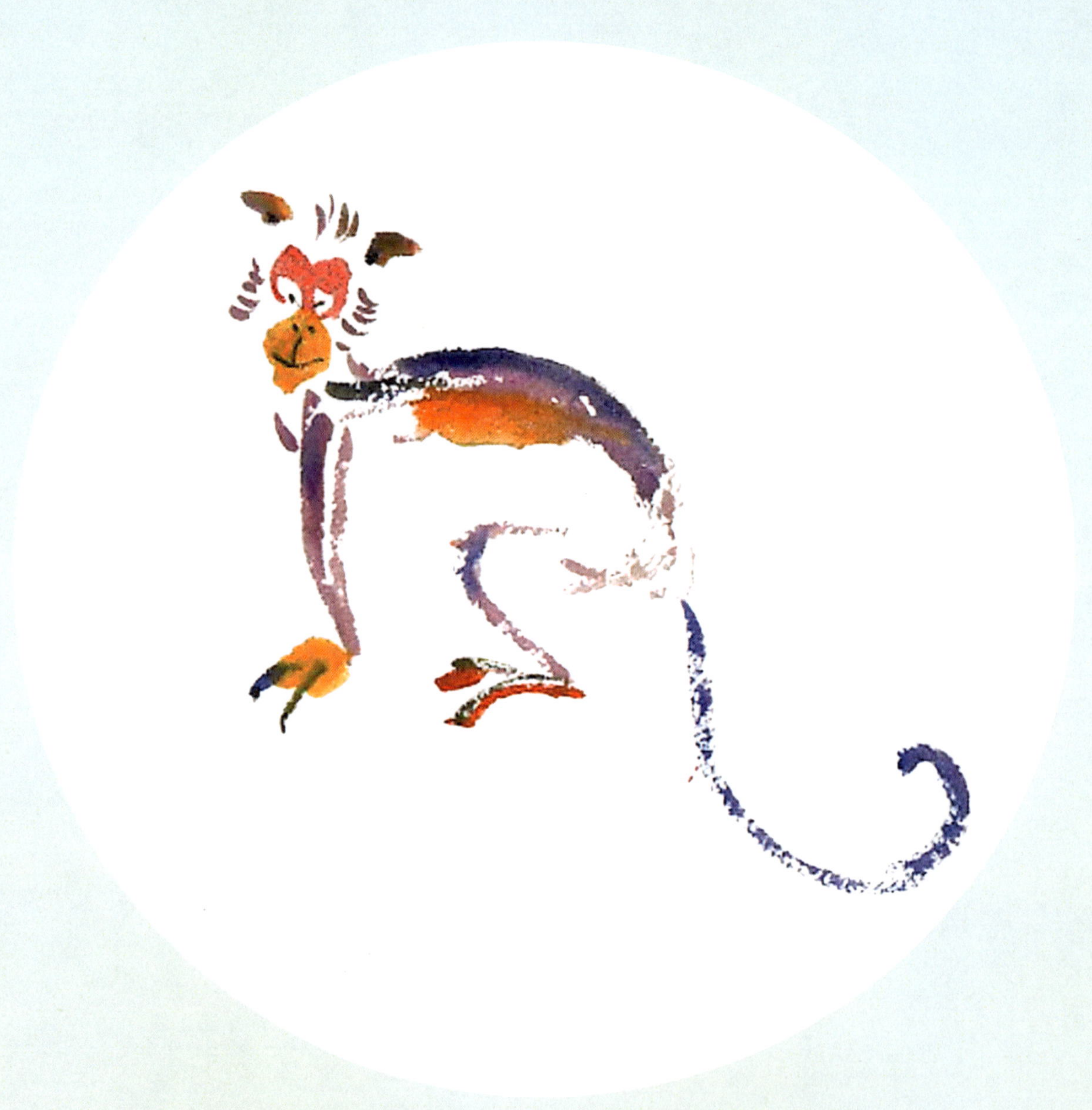

Hóu Monkey

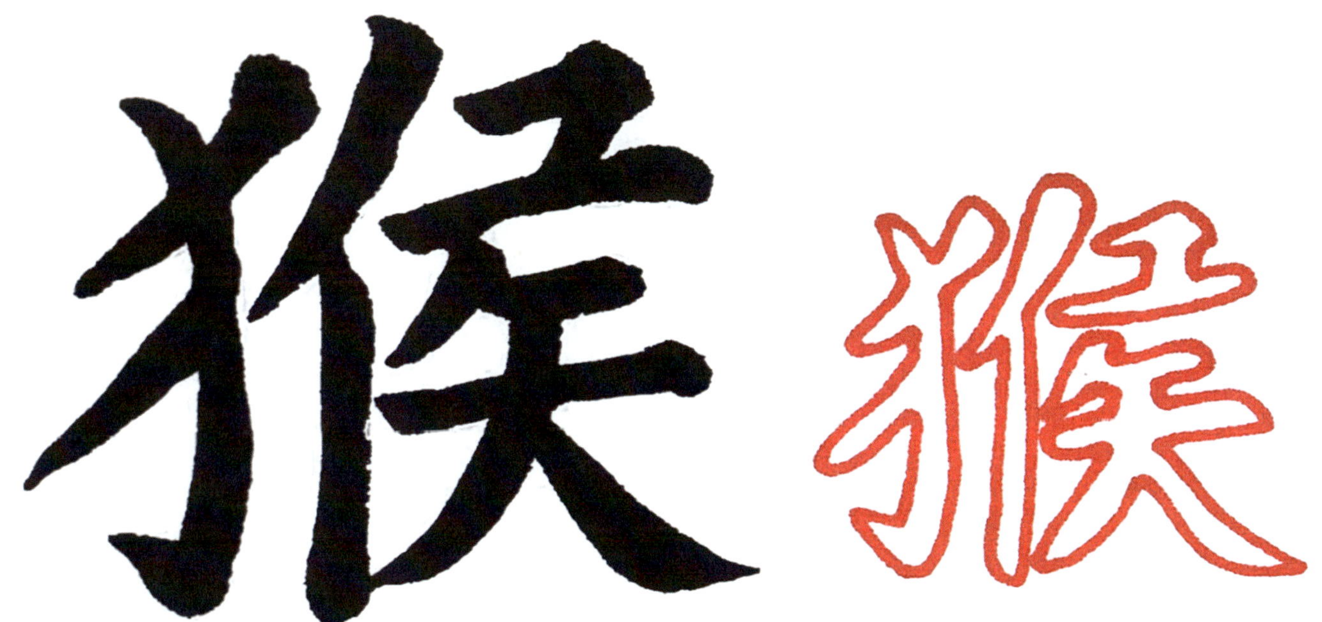

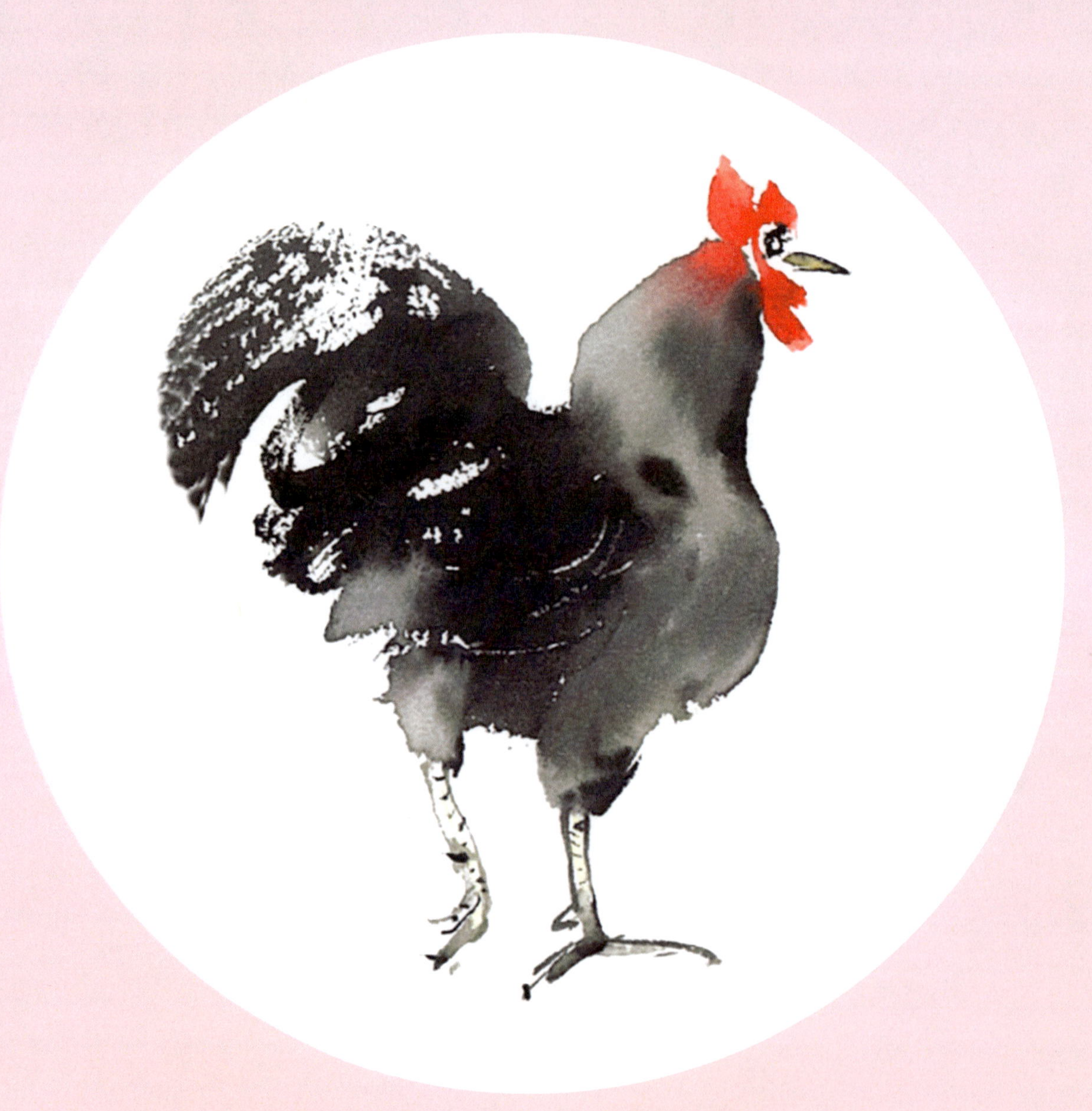

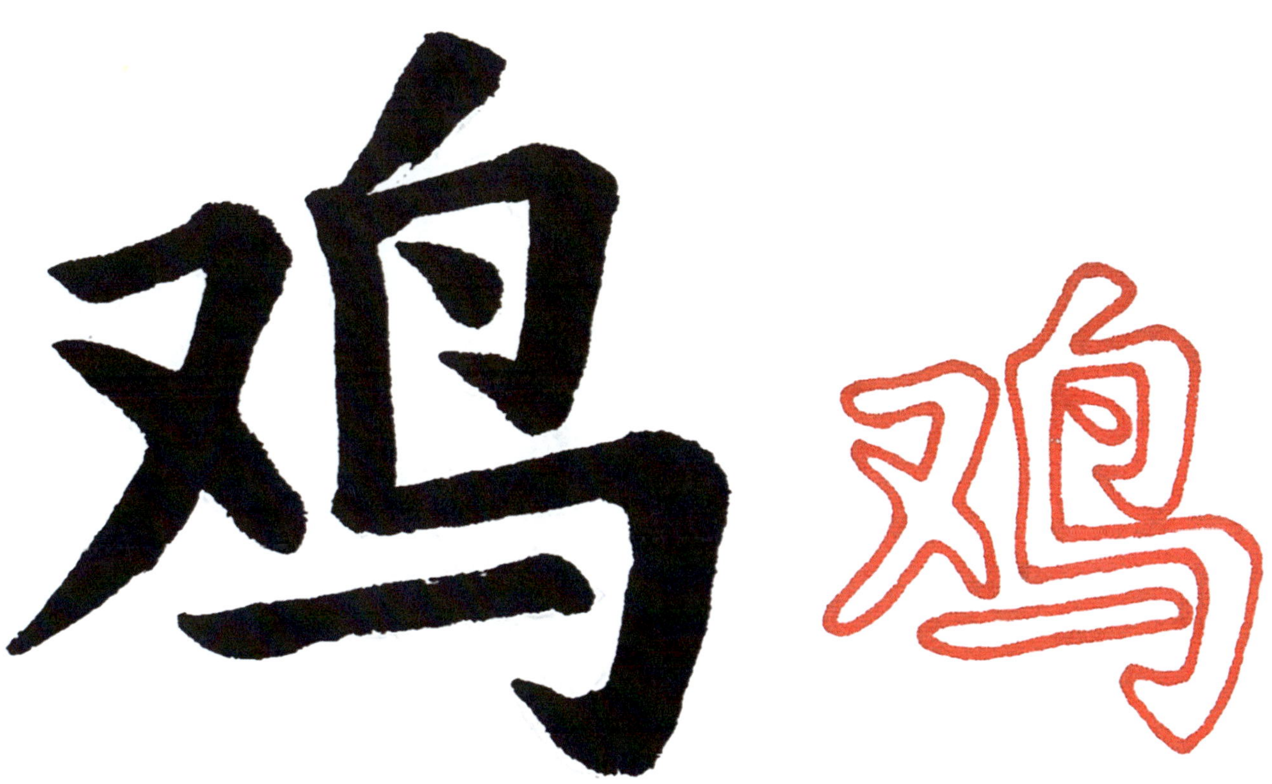

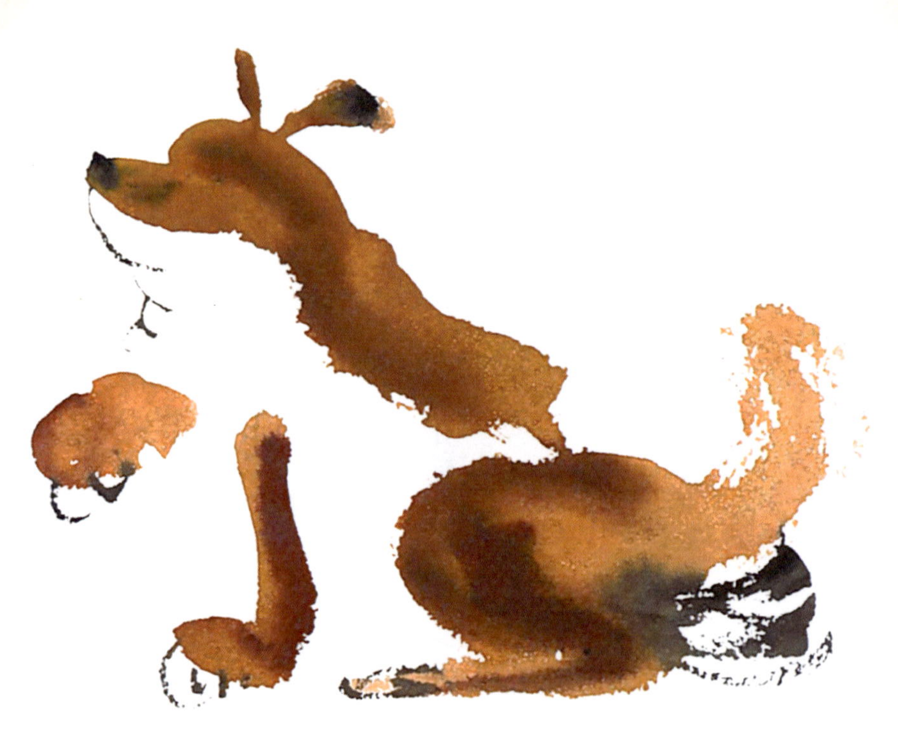

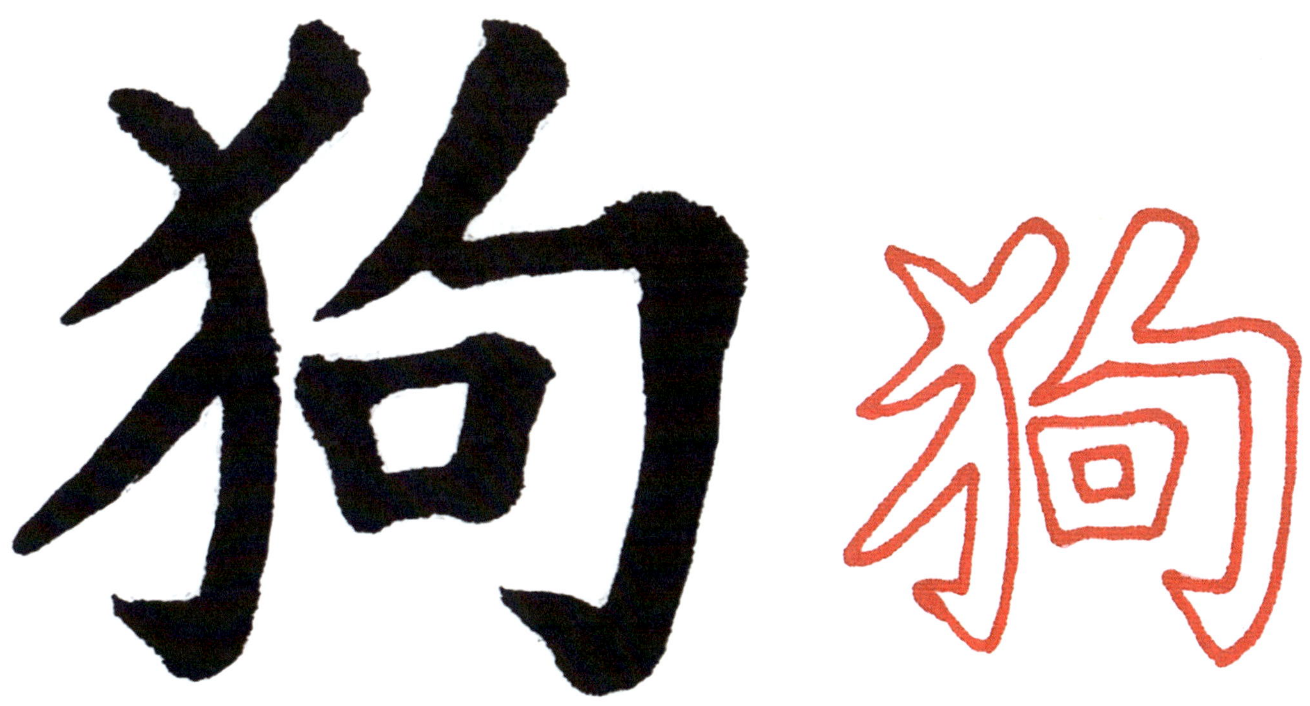

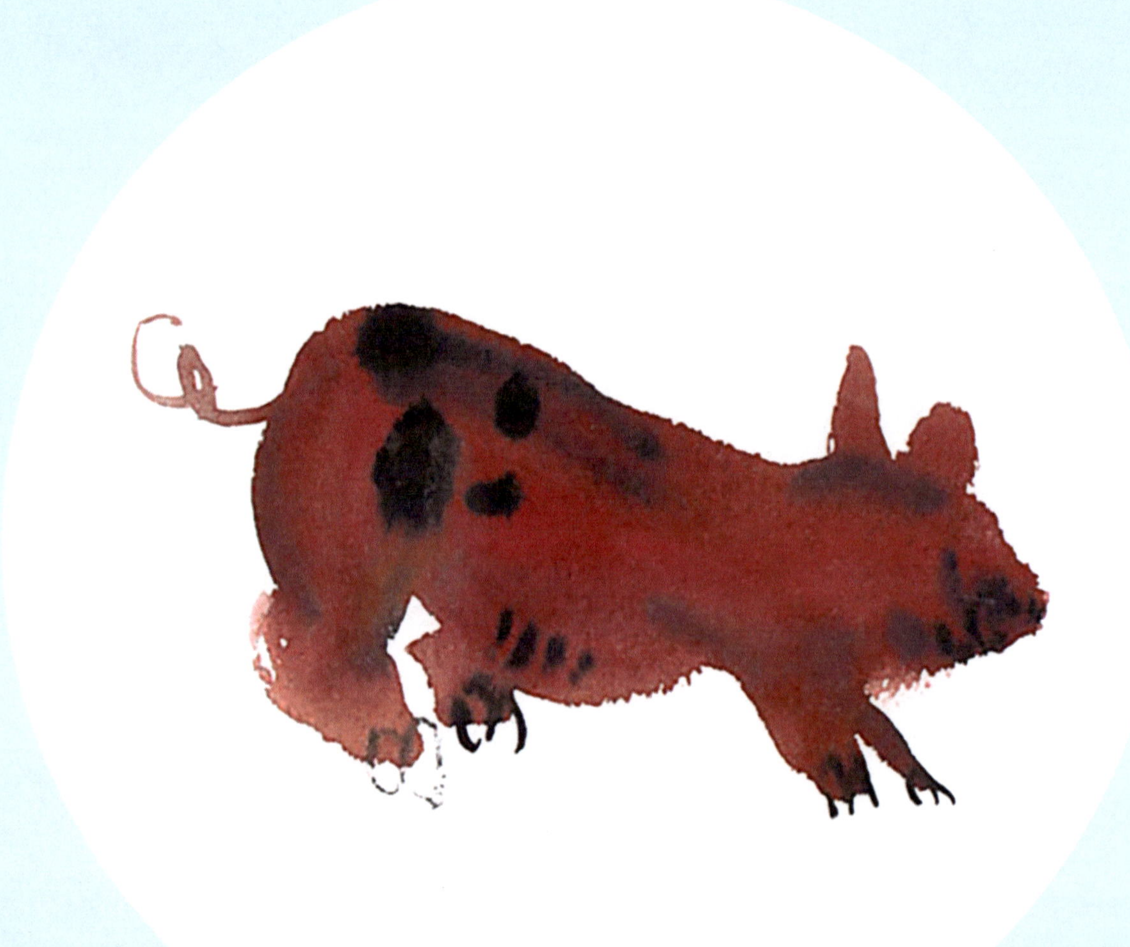

Zhū Pig

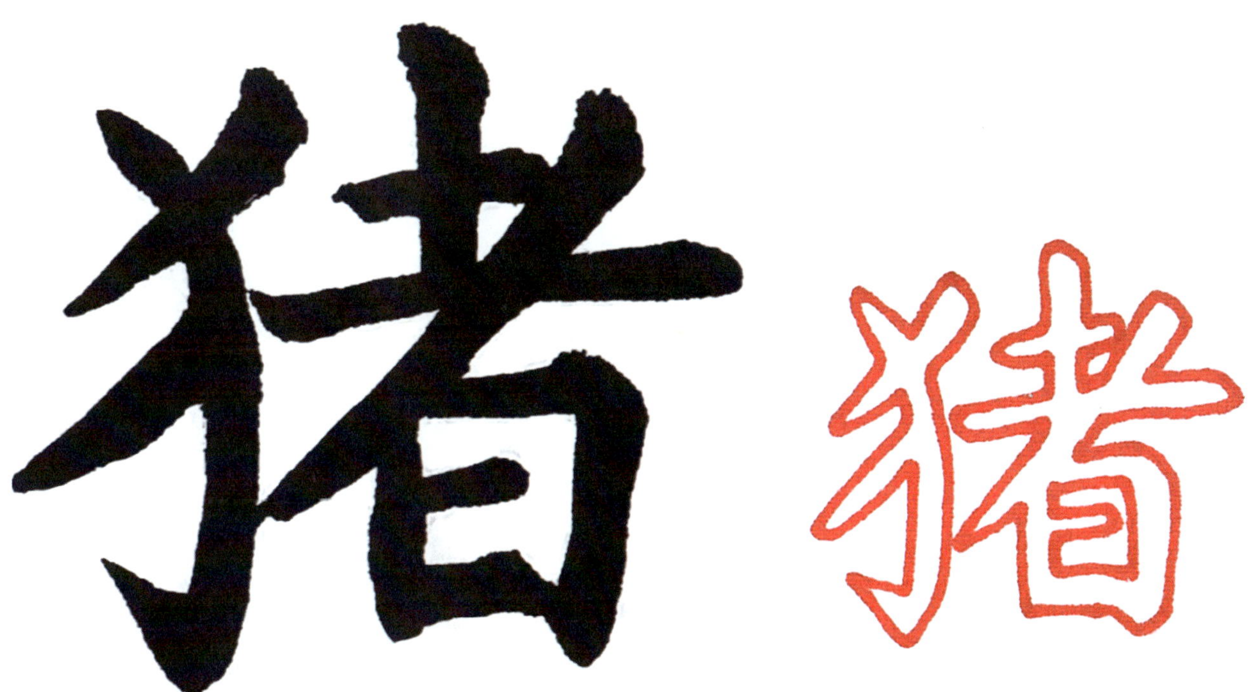

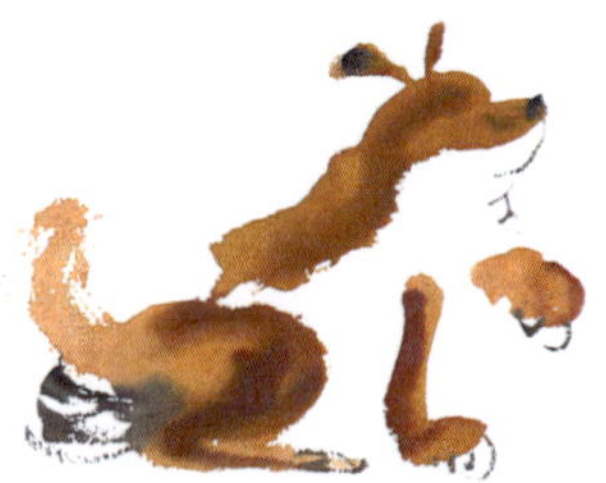
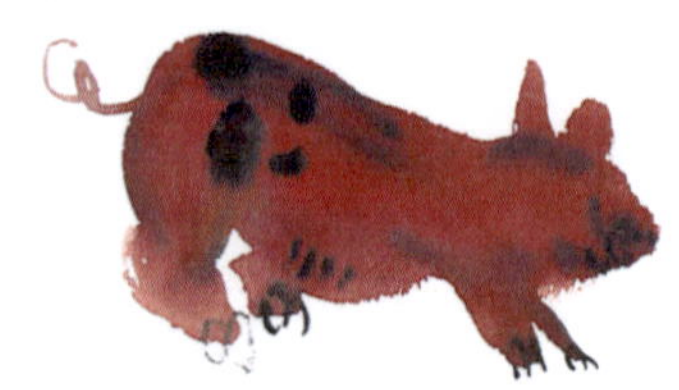
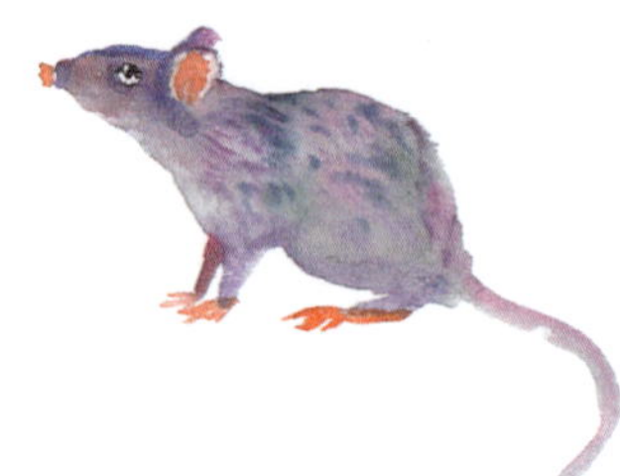

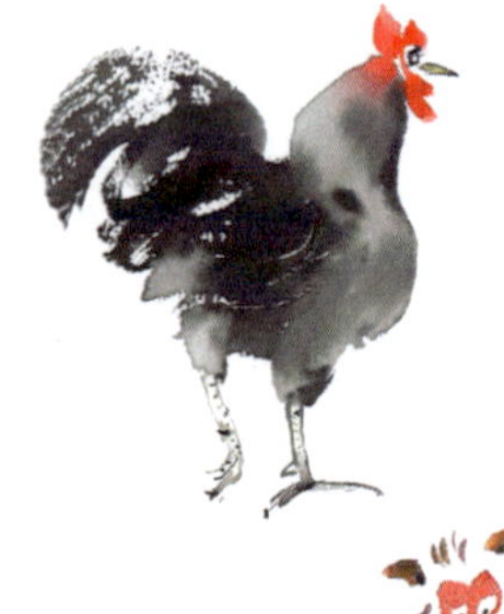
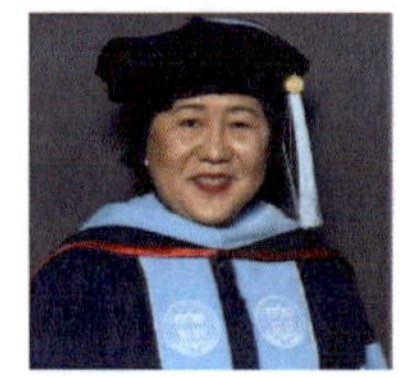
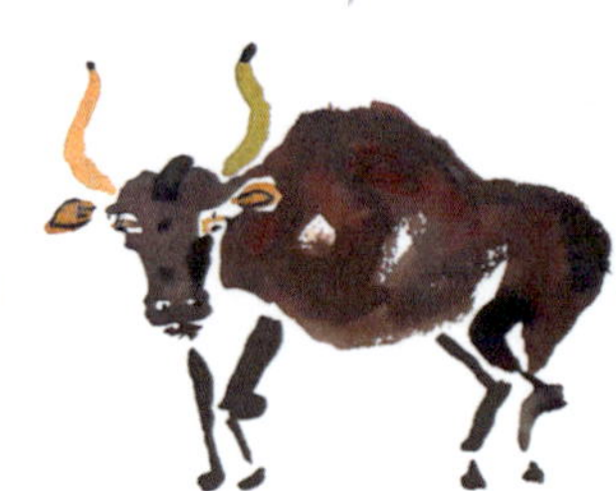

Dr. Ping Xu Moroney brings decades of teaching experience from her roles as an artist and Chinese teacher in schools in both China and America.

This long and varied career has enabled her to develop a powerful, knowledge-rich methodology for learning Chinese, rooted in thousands of years of Chinese art.

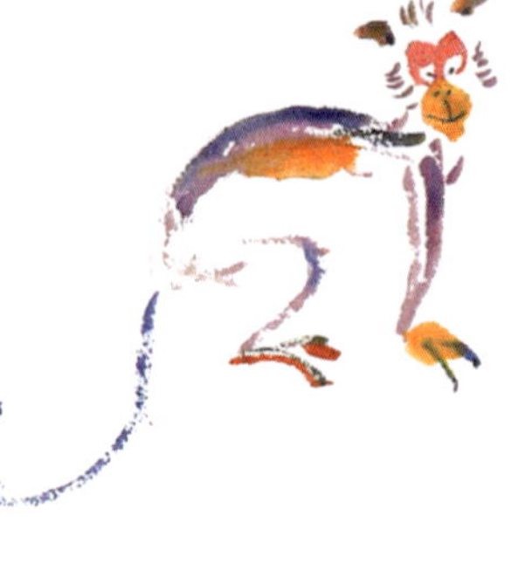
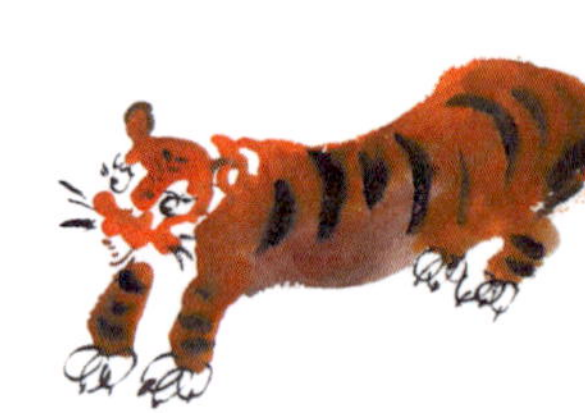

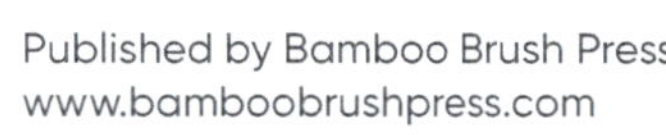
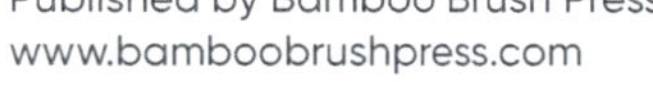
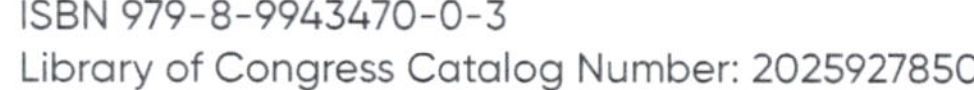
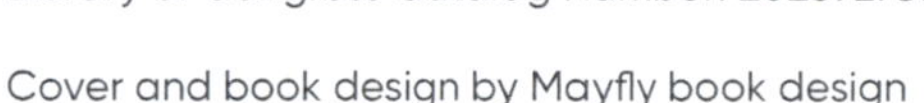

Chinese Zodiac © copyright 2026 by Dr. Ping Xu Moroney. All rights reserved. No part of this book may be reproduced in any form whatsoever, by photography or xerography or by any other means, by broadcast or transmission, by translation into any kind of language, nor by recording electronically or otherwise, without permission in writing from the author, except by a reviewer, who may quote brief passages in critical articles or reviews.

This book was created entirely by human authors without the use of generative AI. No part of this publication may be used in the development, training, or enhancement of artificial intelligence systems without the express written permission of the publisher.

Published by Bamboo Brush Press
www.bamboobrushpress.com

ISBN 979-8-9943470-0-3
Library of Congress Catalog Number: 2025927850

Cover and book design by Mayfly book design
First Printing: 2026

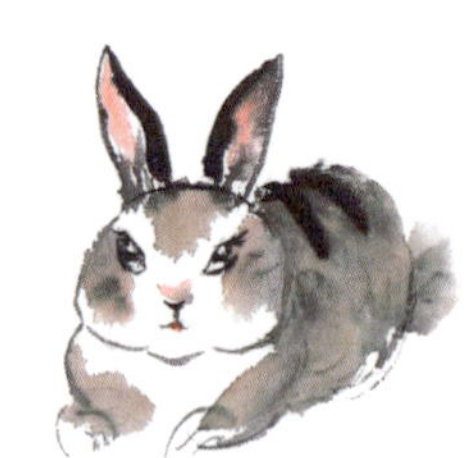

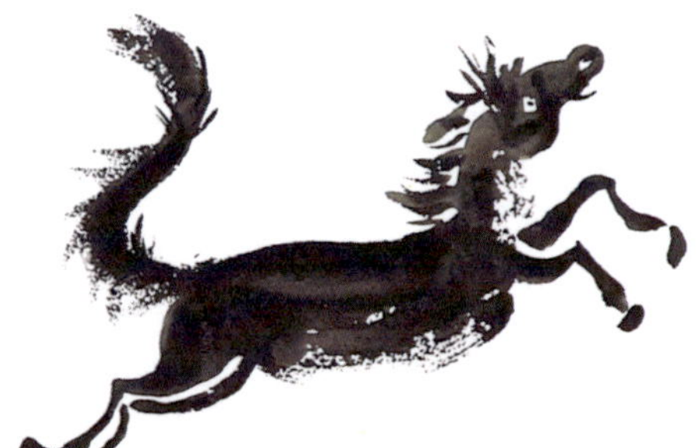
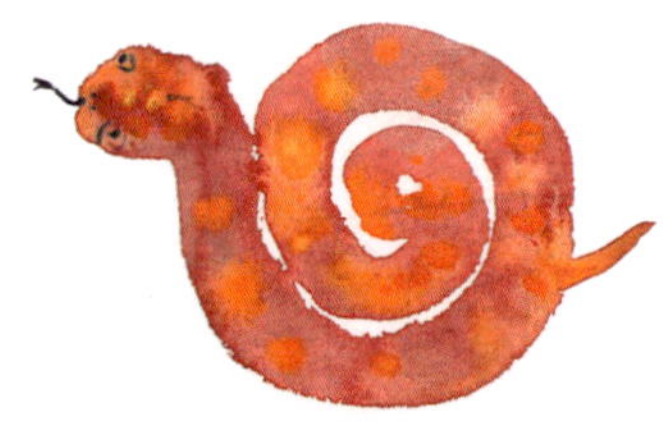
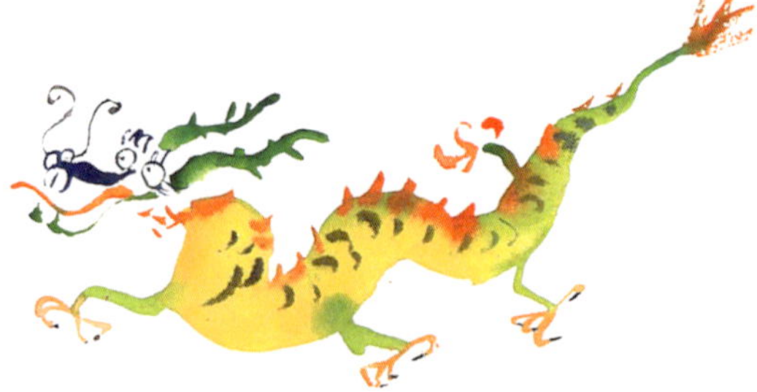

www.ingramcontent.com/pod-product-compliance
Lightning Source LLC
Chambersburg PA
CBRC092051150726
48005CB00031B/1002